LAYERS OF LEARNING

YEAR FOUR • UNIT TWENTY

TERRORISM
AMERICA IN REVIEW
CONSERVATION
CREATIVE KIDS

Published by HooDoo Publishing
United States of America
© 2017 Layers of Learning

(Grilled Cheese BTN Font) © Fontdiner - www.fontdiner.com
ISBN #978-1974580910

Units at a Glance: Topics For All Four Years of the Layers of Learning Program

1	History	Geography	Science	The Arts
1	Mesopotamia	Maps & Globes	Planets	Cave Paintings
2	Egypt	Map Keys	Stars	Egyptian Art
3	Europe	Global Grids	Earth & Moon	Crafts
4	Ancient Greece	Wonders	Satellites	Greek Art
5	Babylon	Mapping People	Humans in Space	Poetry
6	The Levant	Physical Earth	Laws of Motion	List Poems
7	Phoenicians	Oceans	Motion	Moral Stories
8	Assyrians	Deserts	Fluids	Rhythm
9	Persians	Arctic	Waves	Melody
10	Ancient China	Forests	Machines	Chinese Art
11	Early Japan	Mountains	States of Matter	Line & Shape
12	Arabia	Rivers & Lakes	Atoms	Color & Value
13	Ancient India	Grasslands	Elements	Texture & Form
14	Ancient Africa	Africa	Bonding	African Tales
15	First North Americans	North America	Salts	Creative Kids
16	Ancient South America	South America	Plants	South American Art
17	Celts	Europe	Flowering Plants	Jewelry
18	Roman Republic	Asia	Trees	Roman Art
19	Christianity	Australia & Oceania	Simple Plants	Instruments
20	Roman Empire	You Explore	Fungi	Composing Music

2	History	Geography	Science	The Arts
1	Byzantines	Turkey	Climate & Seasons	Byzantine Art
2	Barbarians	Ireland	Forecasting	Illumination
3	Islam	Arabian Peninsula	Clouds & Precipitation	Creative Kids
4	Vikings	Norway	Special Effects	Viking Art
5	Anglo Saxons	Britain	Wild Weather	King Arthur Tales
6	Charlemagne	France	Cells & DNA	Carolingian Art
7	Normans	Nigeria	Skeletons	Canterbury Tales
8	Feudal System	Germany	Muscles, Skin, Cardio	Gothic Art
9	Crusades	Balkans	Digestive & Senses	Religious Art
10	Burgundy, Venice, Spain	Switzerland	Nerves	Oil Paints
11	Wars of the Roses	Russia	Health	Minstrels & Plays
12	Eastern Europe	Hungary	Metals	Printmaking
13	African Kingdoms	Mali	Carbon Chemistry	Textiles
14	Asian Kingdoms	Southeast Asia	Non-metals	Vivid Language
15	Mongols	Caucasus	Gases	Fun With Poetry
16	Medieval China & Japan	China	Electricity	Asian Arts
17	Pacific Peoples	Micronesia	Circuits	Arts of the Islands
18	American Peoples	Canada	Technology	Indian Legends
19	The Renaissance	Italy	Magnetism	Renaissance Art I
20	Explorers	Caribbean Sea	Motors	Renaissance Art II

3	History	Geography	Science	The Arts
1	Age of Exploration	Argentina & Chile	Classification & Insects	Fairy Tales
2	The Ottoman Empire	Egypt & Libya	Reptiles & Amphibians	Poetry
3	Mogul Empire	Pakistan & Afghanistan	Fish	Mogul Arts
4	Reformation	Angola & Zambia	Birds	Reformation Art
5	Renaissance England	Tanzania & Kenya	Mammals & Primates	Shakespeare
6	Thirty Years' War	Spain	Sound	Baroque Music
7	The Dutch	Netherlands	Light & Optics	Baroque Art I
8	France	Indonesia	Bending Light	Baroque Art II
9	The Enlightenment	Korean Peninsula	Color	Art Journaling
10	Russia & Prussia	Central Asia	History of Science	Watercolors
11	Conquistadors	Baltic States	Igneous Rocks	Creative Kids
12	Settlers	Peru & Bolivia	Sedimentary Rocks	Native American Art
13	13 Colonies	Central America	Metamorphic Rocks	Settler Sayings
14	Slave Trade	Brazil	Gems & Minerals	Colonial Art
15	The South Pacific	Australasia	Fossils	Principles of Art
16	The British in India	India	Chemical Reactions	Classical Music
17	The Boston Tea Party	Japan	Reversible Reactions	Folk Music
18	Founding Fathers	Iran	Compounds & Solutions	Rococo
19	Declaring Independence	Samoa & Tonga	Oxidation & Reduction	Creative Crafts I
20	The American Revolution	South Africa	Acids & Bases	Creative Crafts II

4	History	Geography	Science	The Arts
1	American Government	USA	Heat & Temperature	Patriotic Music
2	Expanding Nation	Pacific States	Motors & Engines	Tall Tales
3	Industrial Revolution	U.S. Landscapes	Energy	Romantic Art I
4	Revolutions	Mountain West States	Energy Sources	Romantic Art II
5	Africa	U.S. Political Maps	Energy Conversion	Impressionism I
6	The West	Southwest States	Earth Structure	Impressionism II
7	Civil War	National Parks	Plate Tectonics	Post Impressionism
8	World War I	Plains States	Earthquakes	Expressionism
9	Totalitarianism	U.S. Economics	Volcanoes	Abstract Art
10	Great Depression	Heartland States	Mountain Building	Kinds of Art
11	World War II	Symbols & Landmarks	Chemistry of Air & Water	War Art
12	Modern East Asia	The South	Food Chemistry	Modern Art
13	India's Independence	People of America	Industry	Pop Art
14	Israel	Appalachian States	Chemistry of Farming	Modern Music
15	Cold War	U.S. Territories	Chemistry of Medicine	Free Verse
16	Vietnam War	Atlantic States	Food Chains	Photography
17	Latin America	New England States	Animal Groups	Latin American Art
18	Civil Rights	Home State Study I	Instincts	Theater & Film
19	Technology	Home State Study II	Habitats	Architecture
20	Terrorism	America in Review	Conservation	Creative Kids

Unit 4-20

Printable Pack

This unit includes printables at the end. To make life easier for you we also created digital printable packs for each unit. To retrieve your printable pack for Unit 4-20, please visit

www.layers-of-learning.com/digital-printable-packs/

Put the printable pack in your shopping cart and use this coupon code:

730UNIT4-20

Your printable pack will be free.

Layers of Learning Introduction

This is part of a series of units in the Layers of Learning homeschool curriculum, including the subjects of history, geography, science, and the arts. Children from 1st through 12th can participate in the same curriculum at the same time - family school style.

The units are intended to be used in order as the basis of a complete curriculum (once you add in a systematic math, reading, and writing program). You begin with Year 1 Unit 1 no matter what ages your children are. Spend about 2 weeks on each unit. You pick and choose the activities within the unit that appeal to you and read the books from the book list that are available to you or find others on the same topic from your library. We highly recommend that you use the timeline in every history section as the backbone. Then flesh out your learning with reading and activities that highlight the topics you think are the most important.

Alternatively, you can use the units as activity ideas to supplement another curriculum in any order you wish. You can still use them with all ages of children at the same time.

When you've finished with Year One, move on to Year Two, Year Three, and Year Four. Then begin again with Year One and work your way through the years again. Now your children will be older, reading more involved books, and writing more in depth. When you have completed the sequence for the second time, you start again on it for the third and final time. If your student began with Layers of Learning in 1st grade and stayed with it all the way through she would go through the four year rotation three times, firmly cementing the information in her mind in ever increasing depth. At each level you should expect increasing amounts of outside reading and writing. High schoolers in particular should be reading extensively, and if possible, participating in discussion groups.

These icons will guide you in spotting activities and books that are appropriate for the age of child you are working with. But if you think an activity is too juvenile or too difficult for your kids, adjust accordingly. The icons are not there as rules, just guides.

☺ 1st-4th
☺ 5th-8th
☺ 9th-12th

Within each unit we share:

EXPLORATIONS, activities relating to the topic;
EXPERIMENTS, usually associated with science topics;
EXPEDITIONS, field trips;
EXPLANATIONS, teacher helps or educational philosophies.

In the sidebars we also include Additional Layers, Famous Folks, Fabulous Facts, On the Web, and other extra related topics that can take you off on tangents, exploring the world and your interests with a bit more freedom. The curriculum will always be there to pull you back on track when you're ready.

UNIT TWENTY

TERRORISM - AMERICA IN REVIEW - CONSERVATION - CREATIVE KIDS

No act of kindness, no matter how small, is ever wasted.
-Aesop

LIBRARY LIST

HISTORY

Search for: terrorism, war on terror, 9-11, radicalism, counter-terrorism. It is very difficult to find books on this topic. Most focus on 9/11 and Islamic terrorism. Recent newspapers from your library may be an effective primary source on terrorism.

☺ September 11, 2001: Then and Now by Peter Benoit. Tells lots of facts about that day and some more intimate details of personal stories.

☺ ☺ I Survived the Attacks of September 11, 2001 by Lauren Tarshis. A fictionalized account of the 9-11 attack in New York. Page-turner.

☺ ☺ America Is Under Attack: September 11, 2001: The Day the Towers Fell by Don Brown. Takes events one by one in a factual account of that day.

☺ Ten True Tales: Heroes of 9/11 by Allan Zullo. Inspiring stories of people who went above and beyond. Written for middle grades, but your high schooler may like it too.

☺ ☺ Jihad: Islamic Fundamentalist Terrorism by Samuel M. Katz. Unlike most books on this subject, especially those written for children, this one doesn't sugar coat or excuse the Islamic terrorists, but unapologetically tells the reader they want to wipe you from the face of the earth. For people who want to understand the harsh reality of terrorism. Look for others by this author.

☺ ☺ America Under Attack: September 11, 2001 by Gail B. Stewart. Intense stories of what really happened on that day. Not for the faint of heart.

☺ Terrorism: A History by Randall Law. Puts terrorism in context; ancient to modern.

☺ Terrorism: A Very Short Introduction by Charles Townshend. Indeed, very short at only 176 pages. Covers mostly the definitions and problems of terrorism more than events of terror or terror groups.

☺ Ghost Wars: The Secret History of the CIA, Afghanistan, and Bin Laden, from the Soviet Invasion to September 10, 2001 by Steve Coll. Long, 738 pages, but worth it. Details how the U.S. got involved with and was actually instrumental in putting Al Queda and the Taliban in power, but doesn't cross the line into the blame game. Just the facts.

☺ Because They Hate: A Survivor of Islamic Terror Warns America by Brigitte Gabriel.

GEOGRAPHY	Search for: U.S.A., United States of America, America ☺ America: A Patriotic Primer by Lynne Cheney. ☺ America Is. . . by Louise Borden. ☺ ☻ ☻ The Scrambled States of America by Laurie Keller. ☺ ☻ ☻ America the Beautiful to Paint or Color by Dot Barlowe. This is a coloring book by Dover Publishers that showcases American scenes and scenery. ☺ ☻ ☻ The Children's Book of America by William J. Bennett. This is an audio book with stories and songs featuring America and its culture. ☺ ☻ ☻ America Scratch and Sketch: An Art Activity Book for Adventurous Artists and Explorers of All Ages by Tom Nemmers. This activity book has scratch art and illustrations of American symbols and historical events. A creative approach to reviewing America. ☻ ☻ America Street: A Multicultural Anthology of Stories by Anne Mazer. This book has fourteen stories of immigrant families who came to America. It's a perfect look at how people from many countries have come together to form America.
SCIENCE	Search for: conservation, ecology, recycling, endangered species, pollution ☺ Almost Gone: The World's Rarest Animals by Steve Jenkins. ☺ Conservation by Christine Petersen. ☺ Where Does the Garbage Go? by Paul Showers. Encourages recycling. ☺ See Inside Recycling and Rubbish by Alex Frith. From Usborne. ☺ ☻ The Everything Kids Environment Book by Sheri Amsel. Includes information coupled with experiments and projects. ☺ ☻ Pollution: Problems and Solutions by National Wildlife Federation. ☻ Big Cat Conservation by Peggy Thomas. Focused on the science behind why and how to conserve big cat populations. ☻ The Fight For Conservation by Gifford Pinchot. From the founder of the U.S. Forest Service. Free on Kindle. ☻ A Sand County Almanac by Aldo Leopold. A series of essays on nature and ethics regarding nature. Considered a classic in this field. ☻ Conservation Science: Balancing the Needs of People and Nature by Peter Kareiva and Michelle Marvier. College text book. On the expensive side.
THE ARTS	Search for: art, creativity, art projects. You can peruse the art shelf in the children's non-fiction section at your library for artistic idea books, but primarily, you should find resources that support your kids' creative interests. For example, if your child wants to try stop animation, search for animation books.

HISTORY: TERRORISM

Terrorism isn't new. It's actually been happening in one form or another since ancient days. But the frequency and death toll of terrorists has dramatically increased since 1970 throughout the world. Some terrorism is carried out by private individuals or groups, and some is carried out or paid for by governments.

This is the aftermath of a terrorist attack on a bus station in Baghdad, Iraq in August of 2005. Forty-three people were killed in this attack.

The most numerous and well-funded terrorist groups are found in the Middle East today. This includes groups like the Palestinian Liberation Organization (PLO), Black September, Muslim Brotherhood, Hezbollah, Hamas, Islamic State, and al-Qaeda. These groups are focused primarily on obliterating Israel and removing all western influence from the Middle East. They also specifically target western nations as the most powerful supporters of Israel and for their massive cultural, economic, and political influence on the Middle East.

But there are many other terrorist organizations around the world. The Provisional Irish Republican Army (IRA) had the goal of freeing Northern Ireland from the United Kingdom. The Ku Klux Klan (KKK) in the U.S., though not very active today, targets blacks. The Euskad: Ta Askatasuna (ETA), also known as the Basque Homeland and Freedom group, are intent on creating a separate and independent Basque state in the northern part of the Iberian Peninsula. Abu Sayyaf is a militant Islamic group in the Philippines that wants its own independent state within the

Philippine Islands. The Revolutionary Armed Forces of Columbia (FARC) desires to remake Columbia into a communist state. The Shining Path in Peru is also fighting to impose communism on their country. Ansaru and Boko Haram both operate in Nigeria and have the goal of creating a pure Islamic state ruled by Sharia law. Their targets are mostly Christians. They have killed an estimated 10,000 people since 2002. Boko Haram is particularly despicable as they use child soldiers in their attacks. And finally, there are several terrorist groups operating the Caucasus region of Russia including Islamic International Peacekeeping Brigade and Riyadus, both of which are wanting to create an independent Islamic nation out of the Chechnya region.

Generally, terrorists have political goals that they believe can best be achieved by force, but they don't have the military might to fight and win a conventional war. Instead they use bombings, hostages, executions, assassinations and mass shootings to make their point. They think that if people are afraid, they will capitulate and give in to the demands of the terrorists. In general, terrorists deliberately target civilians and are not averse to killing or maiming innocent people, including children, to further their goals. They may also target government officials and embassies and occasionally attack military targets, though never in a direct confrontation. Terrorists nearly always claim responsibility for their attacks since their goal is publicity for their group and cause.

☺ ☻ EXPLORATION: Timeline
At the end of this unit you will find a printable timeline. Cut apart the squares and place them on a wall timeline or in a notebook.

This timeline only shows a few of the worst terrorism events since 1970. You can't tell from our list, but terrorist attacks have greatly increased in frequency and death toll over the decades. Browse through www.timelineofterrorism.com for a more complete view.

Normally we recommend our timelines for all ages, but this one with its recitation of death is too disturbing for young children, use your judgment with middle grades kids.

☻ EXPLORATION: Defining Terror
People do not agree on the exact definition of a terrorist attack. Make your own checklist of things you think are involved in a terrorist attack. Think about who does the attacking - private people, governments, individuals, or groups. Also think about the method: conventional weapons or unconventional. What about a kidnapping or vandalism where no one dies? Does it matter what the cause is or what the aims are? Does it matter who is attacked

Famous Folks
Between 1865 and 1877 the Ku Klux Klan in the U.S. killed hundreds of southern voting Republicans, black and white, in a calculated campaign of terror to force people to either change their vote or not vote at all.

Since then the KKK and other white supremacist groups have perpetrated and planned attacks on blacks up to the present day.

Klan meeting in 2005

Today's Klansmen have traded in the white hoods for business suits, but they still believe what they always did.

Teaching Tip
This unit mostly focuses on terror, but also covers wars that occurred in the Middle East as these have had a direct impact on terrorism in the region. The Middle East is the area plagued most by terrorist attacks and political instability in the world today. So make sure to help kids draw the connections.

Deep Thoughts

The word "terrorism" in the media and popular vernacular is not the same as when it is used in the courts or by government officials. In the legal system these words have very specific meanings, and to use them often leads to places we do not want to go. For example, in the United States it is easier to prove a "hate crime" was committed than a "terrorist act," and so the official charge will often be "hate crime" to make it easier to convict the perpetrator. There can be other consequences as well. Read about the Foot Hood shootings for more about legalese.

Another consequence can be that if something is deemed a terror attack, this sometimes involves military strikes in retaliation or other action against foreigners.

But both hate crime and terrorism definitions rely on motives instead of outcomes. Do you think it is appropriate for the courts to be concerned with motives in terms of prosecuting crimes, or should only the outcomes be considered? Should people be punished differently depending on *why* they did something?

- military, police, or civilians? Does it have to involve politics to classify as a terrorist attack?

Read these scenarios and talk together about whether each of these is a terrorist attack. These are based on actual events and the event is in parentheses. Do not read the event until you have discussed all of the scenarios.

- A speedboat filled with explosives by a militant group zooms up alongside a military ship and is detonated, killing and wounding sailors. (USS Cole Attack)
- Letters sent by a lone individual containing a deadly biological agent and the words "death to America, death to Israel" are sent to government officials. (Anthrax letter attacks)
- Unknown gunmen drive-by shoot and kill two government officials. (Jan 4, 2017 Quetta, Pakistan)
- A lone anti-abortionist attacks an abortion clinic killing 3 and injuring 9. (Colorado Springs Planned Parenthood attack)
- A bomb is smuggled onto an airplane by a known militant group and detonated midair, bringing the plane down and killing all aboard. (Air India Flight 182)
- A lone man walks into a church and randomly begins to shoot people, killing 9 and injuring 1 in an attempt to start a race war. (Dylann Roof)
- One man is murdered by a lone religious extremist for selling alcohol. (Jan 3, Cairo, Egypt)
- A lone man deliberately drives a truck into a crowd of Muslims outside a mosque, injuring 11 because he hated Muslims. (June 2017, London)
- A series of car bombings by a known militant group kills 56 and injures 120. (January 2017 Baghdad bombings)
- 276 girls are kidnapped from a school and held by a known fanatic group. (Chibok schoolgirls kidnapping)
- A man was stabbed for speaking Arabic. (Jan 5, 2017 Ashod, Israel)

Write your own definition of a terrorist attack in your notebook.

☺ ☺ ☺ EXPLORATION: Mapping Terror

At the end of this unit you will find a map of the world. Color in the countries with dots to show the terrorism hot spots in the world. The map shows the countries where most terrorist attacks occur. The worst of all are in the Middle East and northern and central Africa. Talk about why you think those places have more terrorist attacks than other countries.

Worldwide Terror
Countries with the most frequent terrorist attacks in the early 21st century

Layers of Learning

☺ ☻ **EXPLORATION: The Persian Gulf War**

Iraq was invaded by a coalition of thirty-four nations as a response to Iraq's invasion of Kuwait in 1991. The invading nations were led by the United States.

Watch "Persian Gulf War: Timeline of Operation Desert Storm," a 5 minute history about this war: https://youtu.be/l2TQ8a4LK3A.

As you watch the video, take notes. Divide a sheet of paper into thirds with the paper oriented landscape. Write down causes, or things that led to the war, in the first column. In the middle column, write down events of the war. In the final column, write down the consequences of the war. You will probably want to pause the video often. Use your notes to make a poster about the war.

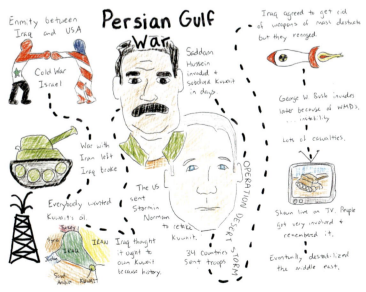

Fabulous Fact

Over time the distribution and frequency of terror can change dramatically. Up until the 1990s, Guatemala, Nicaragua, and el Salvador were riddled with violent terrorist attacks, but today they're mostly peaceful. Before the U.S. unseated Saddam Hussein in 2001, Iraq had very few terrorist attacks, but today it has more than half of the attacks worldwide. Political conditions and other factors, like economics, can greatly affect the level of terrorism in a particular country and also worldwide.

Fabulous Fact

The U.S. has been accused of interfering in the Middle East only because of oil, a stance that is seen as mercenary. What do you think about the importance of oil? Is it worth going to war over? Do you think the U.S. really did go to war just for oil?

Additional Layer

Read up on the Iran-Iraq War of the 1980s. How did that war lead, in part, to the conditions we see in the Middle East today?

On the Web

"Terrorism, War, and Bush 43" from Crash Course is an excellent overview of the George W. Bush presidency and especially the War on Terror for middle grades through high school. https://youtu.be/nl-snnhn3VWE

On the Web

"BOATLIFT, An Untold Tale of 9/11 Resilience" tells the story of some ordinary people who helped on the day the Twin Towers fell. https://youtu.be/MDOrzF7B2Kg. This video has some scary, dramatic parts, so please pre-watch.

For younger kids read *Saved by the Boats* by Julie Gassman.

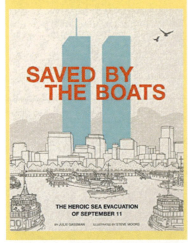

SAVED BY THE BOATS

THE HEROIC SEA EVACUATION OF SEPTEMBER 11

BY JULIE GASSMAN   ILLUSTRATED BY STEVE MOORS

Teaching Tip

"Look for the Helpers" could be adapted to any event or disaster that occurs.

☺ ☺ EXPLORATION: September 11, 2001

Have a discussion about what happened on September 11, 2001 and why. Who is al-Qaeda and who was Osama Bin Laden? Why did they want to attack America? "9/11 Timeline: The Attacks on the World Trade Center in New York City" from the History Channel is a 5 minute recap of the events in New York City on that day: https://youtu.be/GmedslmeiUc. Pre-watch to be sure the video is appropriate for your children. You may also want to watch "Remembering 9/11: The Pentagon Attack," also by the History Channel: https://youtu.be/bNZV8HB8KEU. There was also a fourth plane, not mentioned in these videos, that passengers recaptured from the terrorists, taking the plane down in a field in Pennsylvania.

It is difficult to overstate the importance of the 9/11 attacks to America and to the world at large. In the weeks following the attacks planes were grounded, buildings closed, and financial markets down, all over the world, for days. Military bases, government buildings, and airports went from being fairly open to being closely guarded. Terrorism suddenly became something to fight instead of something that happened in some far off war-torn country. A series of wars were begun that continue to the present day. Most of the Middle East was destabilized and has experienced violence and overthrows repeatedly since then.

Ask three to five adults where they were and what they were doing when they heard the news that the World Trade Center had been struck with planes. What were their thoughts and feelings about the attack at the time? How do they think the attack changed world history? Record or take notes of your interviews. Compile their answers into a book, one section for each question.

☺ ☺ EXPLORATION: Look for the Helpers

Fred Rogers of Mr. Roger's Neighborhood fame said, "My mother would say to me, 'Look for the helpers. You will always find people who are helping.' To this day, especially in times of disaster, I remember my mother's words, and I am always comforted by realizing that there are still so many helpers — so many caring people in this world." So for this exploration focus on the helpers with your children.

Briefly explain the 9-11 attacks to your children. You may want to read a children's storybook or two about the event. Then talk about the heroes who helped both during and after the attacks. Emphasize that only a few dozen were involved in carrying out the attacks, but that millions of people came together to help one another in a time of need.

Firefighters, police, and medical workers rushed to the scene to help the injured and help people evacuate. Thousands of boat operators answered a call from the Coast Guard to rescue people trapped on Manhattan Island. Restaurant and store owners brought food and water to the relief workers. Ordinary people volunteered to help clean up, donate blood and money, and reunite families. HAM radio operators helped rescue workers communicate. Construction workers dropped what they were doing and came with their machines and tools to search for survivors and clean up the rubble. Children wrote letters to the workers to thank them and encourage them. People from all over the world came together to sympathize and help one another.

Make a multi-page book that tells how people helped one another after the attacks. Start with a rectangle of paper, folded in thirds and glued to the center of another sheet of paper. This rectangle forms the body. Then add a round head and a hat, some legs and arms. These can be drawn on or made with paper. Each person you make should represent a different helper. Inside the body section, write how that person helped after the disaster.

☺ ☺ ☺ **EXPEDITION: Memorial**
Visit a memorial to the victims of a terrorist attack. Find out if one is near you. There are memorials to the 9/11 attack all over the United States and the world, not just in Washington D.C. and New York. Learn about the attack and what happened before you go. While you're visiting think about the costs of terrorism and share your thoughts with your family or group.

Additional Layer
Candles are often used in memory of the victims after an attack as well. Make a memorial candle. Start with a white pillar candle. Draw a design on a piece of white tissue paper cut to size. Wrap it around the candle. Wrap a piece of waxed paper over that to use as a handle to hold it while you heat it with a hair dryer. This will melt the outside of the candle and make the design permanently part of the candle.

You can burn the candle normally.

Additional Layer

In 2001, America responded to the violence of the attack on the Twin Towers by going to war. In the end Al Qaeda was weakened and its leader, Osama Bin Laden, was killed, but terrorism was certainly not weakened. More terrorist attacks are happening now than ever before.

In Unit 4-18 we learned how groups and individuals have changed things for the better in their own countries through non-violent means. Is it possible to defeat terrorism though non-violent means? Read this: http://foreignpolicy.com/2016/03/14/how-to-beat-the-islamic-state-through-non-violence/. Do you agree with the author?

On the Web

View a map that shows terror attacks in real time.

https://storymaps.esri.com/stories/terrorist-attacks/?year=2017

Fabulous Fact

It is true that, by far, most attacks today are carried out by militant Islamists. It is also true that most victims are peaceful Muslims.

☻ EXPLORATION: The War on Terror

After the attack on the Twin Towers and so many Americans dying, the Americans went to war. Dozens of nations supported the U.S. with money and troops. It was called the "War on Terror." First, they invaded Afghanistan in their search for Osama Bin Laden, the man who had planned the attacks. Then they invaded Iraq. President George W. Bush said the war would not be over until every terrorist was found and defeated across the globe. Today there are more terrorist attacks than there were in 2001 and more terrorist groups in more countries. Americans have mostly pulled their soldiers back home.

Some people think this war was the right thing to do and stand behind it, while others think it was a terrible mistake. A third group think it was right in the beginning, but that the United States failed to create a proper exit plan and that troops were too long in the Middle East. Read about these points of view. You should be able to find news opinion pieces online by searching for "War on Terror." Make sure you read from more than one point of view. After you read, take a stand and write your own newspaper editorial about why you are for or against the war.

☻ ☻ EXPLORATION: This Is Terrorism

It is important to understand that terrorism happens worldwide and is done by all sorts of people with all sorts of beliefs. The thing terrorists have in common is a fanatical belief that they know what is right and must make everyone else comply with their way. They are willing to do anything for their cause. It is that belief in force that is the problem, not the specific tenets of their faith or political stance.

At the end of this unit you will find a notebooking page. Cut out the title and glue it to the top of the page. Cut out the flaps on the solid lines, fold on the dashed lines, and glue each tab to another sheet of paper.

Each flap has a date and a place on it. Look up the date and place online. You will find news or Wikipedia articles about each attack. Write a sentence giving a brief summary of the attack under the flap. Pay attention to what these terrorists believe in and who they attack.

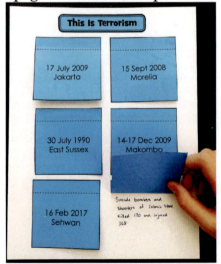

☺ ☺ ☺ EXPLORATION: We Have Flowers

Immediately after a terrorist attack in France, a father was interviewed, comforting his small son. He told his boy, "They might have guns, but we have flowers." You can watch the interview here: https://youtu.be/xkM-SDNoI_8.

The words of the father were profound. Flowers can't physically protect you of course, but as long as there are millions who bring flowers and only few who bring violence, the violence will never really win. The terrorists can only win if they truly make us too afraid to come together in support.

Make a bouquet of flowers from paper and glue. Cut bright or patterned paper into rectangles. Fold it accordion style. Staple in the middle of the folded paper. Fan the sides out and glue together with school glue, forming the flower. Then you can add a large button, a pom pom, or a circle of paper to make the center of the flower. Glue stems made of straws or chenille stems, or punch holes in one edge of each flower and string them together to make a garland.

☺ ☺ ☺ EXPLORATION: Civil Liberties and Safety

Because of the rise in attacks, and especially because of the airplane attacks on 9/11, governments around the world have instituted new programs and security measures to try to prevent terror attacks from happening in the first place. Some of these things include listening in on private conversations on phones, email, and in chat rooms, often without warrants; new agencies like Homeland Security in the United States; and new measures for airport security.

Additional Layer

The War on Terror had the unintended consequence of destabilizing the Middle East and strengthening radical groups, some of them terrorists. This has led to the overthrow of many governments in an overall movement known as the "Arab Spring."

This situation, along with continual fighting with terrorist groups like the Taliban and the Islamic State, have created refugee crises in Syria, Afghanistan, and Iraq, among other places.

Learn about the ongoing refugee problems and what solutions are being talked about or implemented. It helps to read some personal accounts of refugees.

Fabulous Fact

In South and Central America the driving force behind terror is the drug trade, which is frequently used to finance the political goals of communist terror groups.

But in recent years Middle Eastern terror groups like Hamas and al-Qaeda have developed terror cells in Mexico, Venezuela, and other Latin American countries.

Additional Layer

The new uptick in terrorism since 2001 has also renewed debates about immigration, both legal and illegal, across the world. Learn more about this issue.

Writer's Workshop

Write a three paragraph paper comparing and contrasting the Cold War to terrorism.

In the first paragraph talk about how the fears people have about communism and terrorism are the same and different.

In the second paragraph talk about how the methods of the communists and terrorists are the same and different.

In the third paragraph talk about how government responses are the same and different.

Additional Layer

Direct action is a term used to describe non-political avenues of bringing attention to a cause. Direct action can be anything from a picket line or a sit-in to arson or the spiking of trees. Generally, direct action stops short of harming or killing humans, but sometimes direct action groups can cross the line.

Many people say they feel safer because of these measures. Others say that many of the safety measures actually take away civil liberties. Often it seems like we have to choose between safety and freedom. Talk about this problem as a family. Do you really have to choose? Do the government measures that take away freedom make us safer? Even if they do make us safer, is that a good trade to make? You may want to search for information online to help you understand the facts.

At the end of this unit you will find a printable pamphlet called "A Guide to Airport Safety." On the cover it lists the new rules at airports since the early 2000s. The guide specifically refers to rules in the United States. If your country is different, you can hand-make your own pamphlet instead of using the printable. Discuss each rule and talk about whether you think it is a good rule or not. Write your opinions inside the pamphlet. Include illustrations.

☺ ☻ EXPLORATION: Home Grown Terror

In February of 2008, six masked animal rights activist gunmen entered the home of an animal researcher in Santa Cruz, California and assaulted his family members. A few months later two other researchers from the same facility had their cars firebombed.

In March 2008, the Earth Liberation Front burned four multi-million dollar homes in a Seattle area neighborhood because the group felt they weren't sufficiently "green."

White supremacist groups and individuals have systematically planned terror attacks targeting blacks. In October 2008, two white supremacists were arrested after their plan to attack a black high school and kill 88 students, beheading 11 of them, was discovered. The numbers 88 and 11 are significant to white supremacists.

These are just a few of the attacks that have been planned and carried out among radical groups in recent years in the United States. Many of them never make the national news and others are forgotten after a one-day wonder.

Not all terrorists are from far-off hostile nations. But all terrorists do have two things in common. They take their beliefs to extremes and decide to use death and destruction to accomplish their goals.

Think about the proper ways to achieve something you specifically want or a change you would like to see in society, and then write a non-forceful plan to help it happen.

😊 😊 😊 EXPLORATION: Bioterrorism

Bioterrorism is an attack carried out by deliberately infecting people with bacteria or viral diseases. Up to now it has only been used a few times in recent history, and usually those attempts have been failures. But the threat is real, especially as terrorist groups become better funded and their outreach grows.

To prepare for such an attack, agencies like the CDC (Centers for Disease Control) have emergency plans in place. They also provide information to government agencies and individuals, letting them know how they should best handle it if such a thing should happen.

There are three steps for family preparation:

1. Have an emergency plan in place (this is the same for all emergencies).
2. Know where and how to get antibiotics if an attack hits your town.
3. Know the symptoms of the most likely biological agents so you can identify and get help as soon as possible.

Look up more information from the CDC and make a plan for your family.

😊 😊 EXPLORATION: Be A Hero

In the face of something like terrorism a lot of people feel helpless. But there are things you can do. First, don't be afraid. Second, don't ever let the hateful behavior of others make you hateful. Third, be a hero.

Firefighters, police, and ambulance services are the obvious people who help after an attack, but ordinary people also help with rescue, with letters and kind messages, with funds for victims, and in a thousand other ways. All of these people are heroes.

Make puppets from card stock in the shape of people who are heroes after an attack. Talk about what each of those people do to be a hero. Think of ways you can be a hero.

Additional Layer

In April 1995 Terry Nichols and Timothy McVeigh blew up a truck bomb outside the Oklahoma City Federal Building, killing 168 and injuring 800 others.

McVeigh said his methods were effective since it made the government more careful. What do you think? Does terrorism work?

Additional Layer

When the Soviet Union fell in 1990, many nuclear weapons went missing. The Soviet Union's supply of the small pox virus was also insecure. Many people fear those weapons have made their way into the hands of terrorist groups or rogue states.

Writer's Workshop

Write an acrostic poem about a hero.

Each line of your poem should begin with the letters HERO in order.

GEOGRAPHY: AMERICA IN REVIEW

Writer's Workshop

You can put together some of the maps, projects, and printable activities you've worked on all year to create your own book about the United States of America. Put the pages together in a logical order and have them all bound into a book about the states for your homeschool shelf.

Fabulous Fact

The United States has the largest air force in the entire world.

On The Web

Perhaps the most defining part of American culture is that it is a nation of immigrants. Watch this video, *The Immigration History of the United States* by The Daily Conversation, for a 21 minute review of America's history and culture.

https://youtu.be/lBJcqx-I7kas

In this unit do some activities, quizzes, and crafts that help you review what you've learned about the geography of the United States this year.

☺ ☺ ☺ EXPLORATION: Test of the States

Give your kids a blank map of the United States and see how many states and capitals they can fill in (just states for little kids, and the test could be oral). If they miss some, have them study and re-take the test another day. Keep it light. A test is a memorization tool in itself, so treat this one that way. Go through and fill in answers together and keep taking it until they can fill in at least most of the states and capitals without mistakes. You can find a fill in the blank map to test with at the end of this unit.

For an added challenge, have them start with a blank piece of paper and draw the United States and state boundaries from memory. It won't turn out perfect, but if they get the basic shapes and placements of states and can name them and the capitals, that is a memorized map.

☺ ☺ ☺ EXPLORATION: Regions of the United States

Review the regions we've explored all through this year. Color the regional map and as the kids color, have a discussion of some of the facts they remember about these regions. What is the landscape like? What monuments, parks, preserves, or landmarks are found in each region? What are some unique customs or foods of each region?

You'll find a map of the United States at the end of this unit. Use it to color in the regions.

Pacific: Light Blue
 Hawaii
 California
 Oregon
 Washington
 Alaska
Mountain West: Dark Green
 Idaho
 Utah
 Montana
 Wyoming
 Nevada
 Colorado

Plains: Orange
 North Dakota
 South Dakota
 Nebraska
 Kansas
 Minnesota
 Iowa
 Missouri
Heartland: Red
 Wisconsin
 Illinois
 Indiana
 Michigan
 Ohio

Southwest: Yellow
  Arizona
  New Mexico
  Texas
  Oklahoma
Appalachian: Dark Blue
  Kentucky
  Tennessee
  West Virginia
  Virginia
  North Carolina
Atlantic: Pink
  New York
  Pennsylvania
  Maryland
  Delaware
  New Jersey

South: Purple
  Arkansas
  Louisiana
  Mississippi
  Alabama
  Georgia
  South Carolina
  Florida
New England: Light Green
  Vermont
  New Hampshire
  Maine
  Massachusetts
  Connecticut
  Rhode Island

Additional Layer

Using 8" x 8" pieces of paper or white fabric, make America quilt squares. You will draw something that represents America on the quilt square using permanent pens and crayons. If you use fabric, place a cloth over the top of each square and press it with a warm iron to set the crayon. You either tape them together on to a wall as though you are displaying a paper quilt, or sew them together to make a quilt top. A flat sheet makes an inexpensive backing for your America quilt if you choose to sew it.

The United States of America

Fabulous Fact

Did you know there is enough water in Lake Superior to cover all of North America and South America with one foot of lake water? That is, indeed, a GREAT lake.

☺☺☺ EXPLORATION: Feast of America

Plan a big America feast to celebrate the regions and states of America. Choose at least one food from each region. Here's a sample menu:

- Burgers and fries from California
- Hush puppies from the South
- Limeade from Florida
- Baked beans from New England
- Apple pie from the Plains States
- Cheese from the Heartland
- Pineapple from Hawaii
- Chili from the Southwest

Writer's Workshop

Food is really important to Americans. Americans are known for their large portions and diverse flavors. We've tried a lot of American foods this year. What are your favorite foods from America? Write about them.

On the Web

This site has an adorable colorful map of the United States to make into a jigsaw puzzle: https://mrprintables.com/printable-map-of-the-united-states.html

Additional Layer

You can design an American calendar to learn about American holidays, seasons, or traditions. Use the blank calendar printable from the end of this unit. Print off twelve copies, one for each month. Write the names of each month in the top boxes, then add the dates and the American holidays. Finally, color a picture in the blank area that represents something we celebrate or see in America during that month, like a jack-o-lantern in October or fireworks in July. Add a top binding to your calendar.

You might also find music that goes with each region - grunge from the Pacific Northwest, rap from the big cities, country western from the Midwest and South, jazz from the South, gospel from the South, theater music from New York, movie soundtracks from California, and so on.

☺ ☺ ☺ EXPLORATION: American Landscape

Use the outline map of the U.S.A. from the end of this unit. Have your kids fill in as many mountain ranges, lakes, rivers, deserts, swamps, forests, grasslands, natural landmarks, and man-made landmarks as they can from memory. Can they place Washington D.C. in the right spot on the map?

☺ ☺ EXPLORATION: Is it in America?

At the end of this unit you will find printable landmarks. Cut them apart and have the kids draw the cards one at a time from a pile. They have to decide if it is in America or not. If it is, you should find the location of the landmark on a map of the United States.

The Shanghai Tower, Angel Falls, and St. Peter's Basilica are not in America.

☺ ☺ ☺ EXPLORATION: American Animal Charades

Play a game of charades. Write the names of American species of animals on small slips of paper. Kids can draw them out one by one and try to act out the animal while the rest guess what it is. Here are a few animals found in the United States to get you started: alligator, bald eagle, gray wolf, grizzly bear, moose, prairie dog, deer, elk, chicken, mountain goat, bison, raccoon, blue jay, manatee.

☺ ☻ ☻ EXPLORATION: Paper Landscape Map

Use the free printable landscape papers at MrPrintables.com to craft a landscape map of the United States. https://mrprintables.com/my-paper-world-wild-green.html

☺ ☻ ☻ EXPLORATION: U.S.A. Speed Scavenger Hunt

Give your kids a list of ten places or landmarks and a map of the United States. On their own blank map of the U.S. they have to mark the places or landmarks. The first one done wins, or you can time them to see how fast they can go. Play several times. You can also have them each make a list and then swap lists with one another.

☺ ☻ ☻ EXPLORATION: U.S.A. Bingo

Play U.S.A. Bingo. Use the Bingo cards from the geography printables page at Layers-of-Learning.com. You'll also need small markers, like buttons or pieces of cereal, to mark your Bingo sheet.

The caller calls out the name of a state and the kids search for that state's outline and mark it on their Bingo sheet. The first player to get five in a row in any direction wins! If kids need help, you can give extra clues like. "It's one of the purple ones on your board," or, "It has a peninsula."

United States of America

BINGO

FREE

Layers-of-Learning.com

Fabulous Fact

Did you know there's a basketball court on the 5th floor of the Supreme Court Building in Washington D.C.? It is sometimes called the "highest court in the land."

Additional Layer

For another way to review states, have a state scavenger hunt. Print out the Postal Code Matching Game from Layers-of-Learning.com, and cut apart the cards.

Keep only the state cards with the pictures of each state. Hide the pictures all over the house. On your signal, your kids will begin scouring the house in search of states. Each time they find one, they must come back and find it on the map before going out to search for another state. They will compete against other players to see who can find and locate the most states.

https://layers-of-learning.com/us-postal-codes/

Teaching Tip

We keep this 20 Questions box handy and use it frequently to introduce a new topic. I place something related to our unit into the box. The kids take turns asking yes or no questions while working together to try to solve the puzzle of what is in the box. For example, if I were studying about conservation, I might put a tiny toy dinosaur in the box. The kids ask 20 Questions, all the while trying to guess what it is. That gives us a fun platform for a discussion about extinction and our stewardship over the earth. A simple game keeps their attention and creates a lasting memory that helps them recall the concept we discuss afterward.

Famous Folks

Here are some famous Americans you may want to put on your dollar bill:

Amelia Earhart

Martin Luther King Jr.

Neil Armstrong

Oprah Winfrey

Elvis Presley

Abigail Adams

Rosa Parks

Thomas Edison

EXPLORATION: State Twenty Questions

One person chooses a state. This game works best if you have a large map hanging up in front of everyone, but you could also use small maps or atlases for each person if you don't have a wall map of the United States. Write down the state chosen and put it into an envelope or box. Everyone takes turn asking yes or no questions about the state the person chose, trying to narrow it down and guess the state. In order to win, the guessers must work together to guess the correct state within only twenty questions.

"Is it touching an ocean?" "Is it a plains state?" "Are there mountains running through the state?" "Was it one of the thirteen original colonies?" "Does it have a tropical climate? Does it snow a lot there?"

Keep asking until the state is guessed or you have asked your twenty questions, then it's a new person's turn to pick another state and answer questions.

EXPLORATION: Famous Face on a Dollar Bill

Use the Dollar Bill printable from the end of this unit. Choose a famous American who you think should have his or her face featured on a dollar bill. Currency features people of honor who have contributed to our nation in a considerable way. Draw the person's head in the center of the bill. Write about the accomplishments of the person that made him or her a candidate for the next currency.

EXPLORATION: Melting Pot

Because America is young and is a place where many people from many countries and cultures have gathered, it is a very diverse country. We sometimes call it a melting pot since we've come from all over, but have melted into one country.

Draw a picture of a melting pot, or giant cauldron. Give it the title, "America: A Melting Pot." Then draw or write down things that have been brought to America from other countries. What music, sports, dances, foods, clothing, holidays, languages, animals, religions, and other cultural aspects have been brought to America from other places?

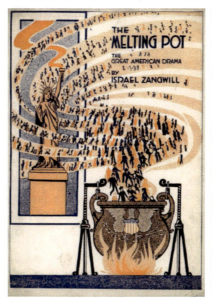

☺ ☺ ☺ **EXPLORATION: Cities of America Alphabet Race**
On a sheet of paper, write down each letter of the alphabet, with one letter on each line. On the signal, all of the kids will race to fill in their puzzles by finding U.S. cites that begin with each letter. Try to be the first one to find and write down all of the cities. Some of them you may be able to think of on your own - A is for Albany, New York. But some are tougher. Did you know about Xanadu, Utah? You'll need the internet for this game in case there are some letters that you can't come up with in your head. Make sure that you write down which state each of the cities is in too.

☺ ☺ **EXPLORATION: American Symbols Mobile**
Make a mobile of things that represent America to you. It could be the Statue of Liberty and the American flag or just apple pie and a baseball game. Maybe fireworks make you think of America, or perhaps it's just a pair of blue jeans. It could even be the Rocky Mountains, the Everglades, or the Hollywood sign. It doesn't matter what you pick as long as it means something for you. Trace canning jar lid circles on to white card stock, twice as many as you have lids. Draw one of the symbols of America on each circle, and then cut out the circles. Attach the paper circles to both sides of canning jar lids.

Use a hammer to pound a nail through one edge of the lid, creating a hole to put a string through. Loop a string through the hole and fasten it to an embroidery hoop or a wire hanger that has been bent into the shape of a circle, with the lid hanging down from the circle. Repeat with each lid, adding all the pieces together to make a mobile that represents America.

Teaching Tip

You can combine the learning styles of your kids by approaching explorations in varied ways. For example, if you discuss the idea of America's melting pot, your auditory and verbal learners will thrive. By making illustrated notes, you can reach your visual and kinesthetic learners. Combining a sketch or doodle with note taking reaches many kids who struggle to remember things. Whenever possible, approach an exploration with your kids' learning style in mind.

Writer's Workshop

Imagine what it would be like to be the President of the United States of America. Write all about the changes you would make in America. What new laws would you help create? Would you designate any new national parks? One of the cool jobs of the president is declaring holidays (Congress has to confirm them as well). What new holiday would you declare? What would you tell your staff to fix for dinner? Where would you go in Air Force One? Write all about your life as the president.

SCIENCE: CONSERVATION

Fabulous Fact

The Hawaiian Goose, also known as the nene, is endemic to the Hawaiian Islands. Hunting and introduced predators reduced the population to just 30 birds by 1952. It was brought back from the brink of extinction by the WWT Slimbridge and Peter Scott in England. The population is now at around 2500 birds, which are protected in Hawaii.

Photo by Jörg Hempel, CC by SA 3.0, Wikimedia.

Additional Layer

Leave No Trace is an outdoor ethic, one that encourages people to use and enjoy the wild lands but not harm them. It is embraced by the National Park Service, the Boys Scouts of America, the Girl Scouts of America, and many other groups. You can learn more here: https://lnt.org/

Look for their online Awareness Course for which you and your kids can earn a certificate.

Conservation is a specific focus within ecology. It is the science of keeping natural environments healthy. It involves species populations, water cleanliness, air cleanliness, and responsible human use of resources.

In the modern day of factory power, huge machinery, chemical advances, and rapid transportation, people are more able than ever before to affect the natural world we live in. So while there's nothing wrong with using the world's resources, if we're not careful, we can do unintended and severe harm to the soil, the water, the air, the plants, and the animals that make up this world. So the goal of conservation is to learn to use the resources we need without destroying the source of them, the natural world. Responsible use of resources benefits not only animals and plants, but also people. We want a clean, beautiful, and healthy world to live in as much as any other living thing on earth.

☺ ☺ ☻ EXPEDITION: Get Outside

The more you spend time in the wilderness, the more you understand and appreciate the natural world. So take a trip to the wild.

While you're on your day trip or camping trip, take lots of photos of the beautiful natural world you find. When you get back home, put them all into a scrapbook or create a slide show with them. Insert captions that remind you of why the world is such a wonderful place and why we should take care that it stays that way.

☺ ☺ ☺ EXPERIMENT: Animal Survey

Choose a category of animals like butterflies, ants, birds, rodents, mammals, fish, or another that is reasonably frequent in your area. Even if you live in the city there are animals, especially birds and bugs. Don't use domestic animals like dogs or cows.

For two weeks you are going to pick a particular location and keep track of all the species of that category of animal that you see in that spot at a particular time of day (or it could be all day).

For example, if you choose to survey all of the birds you see in or near your back yard, you would keep an eye on the windows and write down every species of bird that you spot. You will record the species, the date and time that you saw it, the number of individuals (like if it's a flock of nine geese, you would record that there were nine), and what they were doing when you saw them. If you notice the same flock or individual returning day after day, record that as well. Be as detailed as you can in your observations. You will probably need an animal identification guide to help you in this. Have one on hand at the beginning of the project.

You can do the same thing for fish in a stream, catching them in a net in a particular spot at the same time of day every day for two weeks. Release them as soon as you identify what they are. You may observe butterflies in the backyard, or all the creatures in a particular tide pool, or all the starfish on a particular stretch of beach, or all the snakes in a field, or whatever your environment lends itself to. Be sure you follow the law in your area.

After you complete your survey, compile your observations in a paper with graphs, tables, maps, and illustrations as needed.

☺ ☺ ☺ EXPLORATION: Endangered Species

Some animals and plants are in danger of their entire species dying out. Usually this is a natural process. Species have been going extinct in large numbers throughout the history of the earth. But more and more extinctions are being caused or hastened by people who destroy habitats through encroachment, destruction, introduction of non-native species, or pollution.

Look up threatened and endangered species in your corner of the world. Make a map of the range of this species, previously and currently. Learn what factors have caused the decline of the species. Find out what is being done for conservation or recovery of the species. Put your information on a sheet of card stock and make a mini-poster that you can put in your notebook. You can do this for several different species if you would like.

Fabulous Fact

Animal and plant surveys are important for conservation biologists to do because they can't know whether a species is endangered or healthy if they don't have a count. Doing surveys like this repeatedly over time helps conservationists to understand how populations change when something new happens. What happens to the population of woodpeckers after the new housing development is built? Do they die off, move, or stay put among the houses? You must have a count to determine the condition.

Fabulous Fact

The heath fritillary nearly disappeared from Great Britain by the year 2000.

It has been reintroduced from European populations and efforts are ongoing to protect and expand its habitat.

Photo by Darius Baužys CC by SA 3.0, Wikimedia.

Writer's Workshop

If you live too far from a zoo to take a trip, write to a zoo conservationist with a few questions you have about how the zoo researches or restores animal populations.

Be sure you read their website first so you're not asking questions that have already been answered on the site.

Interested kids might also ask how to become a zoo conservationist.

On the Web

Watch "Is There Hope for Conservation?" from TEDx Talks: https://youtu.be/_lJg4GEjj6M

It's important to understand how people harm the wild, but it is equally important to understand that there is hope.

Famous Folks

Aldo Leopold was an early conservationist who developed an outdoor ethic that we still follow.

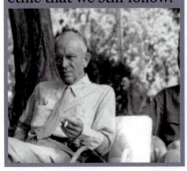

In Idaho, where we live, the bull trout, the only native species of trout in Idaho, is endangered because non-native species of trout were introduced and the streams it lives in have been polluted with silt. The species is being protected and its habitat is being restored. It has already recovered partially.

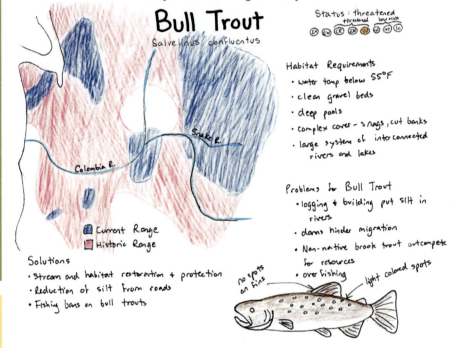

Bull Trout
Salvelinus confluentus

Status: threatened

Habitat Requirements
- water temp below 55°F
- clean gravel beds
- deep pools
- complex cover - snags, cut banks
- large system of interconnected rivers and lakes

Problems for Bull Trout
- logging & building put silt in rivers
- dams hinder migration
- Non-native brook trout outcompete for resources
- over fishing

Solutions
- Stream and habitat restoration + protection
- Reduction of silt from roads
- Fishing bans on bull trouts

Current Range
Historic Range

Colombia R.
Snake R.

no spots on fins
light colored spots

☺ ☺ ☺ EXPEDITION: Go To The Zoo

If there is a zoo or aquarium within driving distance, consider taking a trip there during this unit. Just seeing the animals is fun, but step it up a notch if you can. See if the zoo has conservation lessons or workshops for your kids' age groups. If they don't, see if you can arrange to talk with one of the zoos conservationists. Find out about the zoo's breeding programs and if they're involved in restoring wild populations of endangered animals.

Zoos used to get all their animals from the wild and then exhibit them as curiosities for visitors. They still exhibit animals of course, but zoos have changed their focus from entertainment to education and research. Zoos today usually breed their own animals or buy them from other zoos that breed their animals. Zoos are also engaged in researching animals and their natural habitats and in restoring animals to the wild among populations that are threatened. Ask your zoo conservationist how they do this.

☺ ☺ ☺ EXPERIMENT: Trash, Trash, Trash

Modern households produce lots and lots of trash. The trash often ends up in landfills. A big hole is dug and trash that was collected from households and stores is dumped into the hole. In well-run landfills the trash is covered up every day with a layer of soil or wood chips to keep vermin down. Eventually the landfill is full. Sometimes the land is then reused for development. But underneath, what has happened to all that trash? Some of it certainly decomposes, but does it all? How long does that take?

Do an experiment to see how long it takes to decompose some of your trash. Choose five different items of trash, things you often throw away. Bury them underground in a trench. Mark the places you've left them with labeled craft sticks. Predict how decomposed you think each item will be at the end of the experiment. Then leave them for 4-6 weeks. Longer is better. At the end of your time, dig them up and observe how much they have decomposed. Create a scale like this: 1 - no decomposition; 2 - some holes, beginnings of decomposition; 3- lots of holes, about halfway to decomposition, 4 - mostly decomposed; 5 - completely decomposed. Write about your findings.

☺ ☺ ☺ EXPLORATION: Recycling

Find out which items can be recycled in your city and how to go about it if you don't already know. Create a recycling station at your house to make it easy to recycle the recyclables. If it isn't easy, it won't ever be automatic and you won't stick with it.

Recycling station ideas:

- Line up several identical bins, one for each type of item, and have your kids create illustrations on sheets of paper showing which kind of item goes in each bin. Laminate the papers and attach them to the bin or to the wall above the bin. This works well inside a garage or utility room.

- Buy a pull-out shelf mechanism from a hardware store and install it under your kitchen sink or another cabinet. You can fit two or three medium size trash bins on one roll out shelf.

Fabulous Fact

Sometimes just because it's garbage to you, it may not be to someone else. Before you dump old clothes, appliances, or electronics in the trash see if you can give them to a thrift store or give them away on Freecycle. com.

Expedition

Take a trip to a landfill or a recycling center to learn more. Go prepared with research done and questions ready.

Fabulous Facts

The American bison used to roam in enormous herds over most of North America. Then, in the 1800s, they were hunted nearly to extinction. Only 541 remained in the wild.

Ranchers gathered up some of the few remaining herds and began to breed and protect them. Later the herds were protected by federal law and government agencies. Today there are about 530,000 individuals, most of them living on preserves or farms.

Additional Layer

If you live in the middle of a huge city it can be tempting to believe that the whole world is polluted and all the trees are disappearing. But if you get out into the wilderness you'll find millions of acres of untouched land right in the United States. You'll also find that more of those acres are covered in trees than were one hundred years ago.

The sky is most definitely not falling when it comes to our environment. But being outside also helps you realize how important it is to care for the world.

We definitely do have behaviors we need to change and problems we need to address, but keep it in perspective. Nature is incredibly resilient.

Read this 2009 report from Yale to see how even severely polluted environments can recover: https://news.yale.edu/2009/05/27/most-polluted-ecosystems-can-recover-new-study-finds

The Chernobyl nuclear disaster in 1986 absolutely destroyed the environment. Find out what is going on there now.

Label each bin with the type of recyclable (or trash).

- Stackable shelf bins work well for a recycling center in a mudroom or laundry room. Again, have the kids label or decorate the bins to show what goes where.

Remember, some things that can be recycled don't fit in a bin. Cardboard boxes and automotive oil won't go in your recycling bin but should still be recycled. Make sure you have a place for these things too.

Having the kids involved in planning, installing, and decorating or labeling your recycling area will make them more invested in the concept and foster more cooperation.

☻ ☻ EXPLORATION: Sustainability

Sustainability means that we use today's resources wisely so that the world will still be lovely and abundant for future generations. It includes a high standard of living and the goal of raising the standard of living for the world's poorest people. So it's not about deprivation or going back to the stone ages. It's about living well.

The concept of sustainability is still pretty new, and people are far from agreed on what it really means and how to achieve it. Remember that ecology is a very new and very complicated science. We also are in the infancy of developing technologies that are less harsh on the environment like renewable energy sources. So it's going to take some time and probably lots of mistakes before we even come close to figuring it out. But in spite of this, many people are already moving forward to try to impact the earth less, to change their lifestyles so they consume less and give more.

Look up information on what people are doing to make their lives and neighborhoods more sustainable for the future. Print pictures you find online. Paste them on a sheet of paper and next to them write a few sentences about what each one represents.

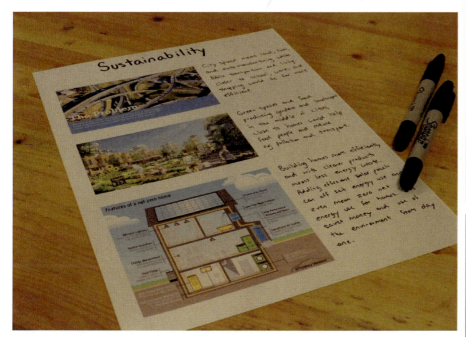

☺ ☻ EXPLORATION: Water Conservation

Water is not scarce on earth. It is one of our most abundant resources, in fact. But water can be scarce in certain places, and clean water can be even more scarce.

If you live in a desert like Phoenix, Arizona, the Australian Outback, or Las Vegas, Nevada, you need to be more aware of your water consumption than if you live in the Great Lakes region, Scotland, or Norway. But in most places, whether there is a lot of water or a little, only a small portion of water is clean and can be used for drinking, bathing, cooking, and so on. It also takes energy to deliver clean water and take care of waste water.

For one full day, keep track of exactly how much water your family uses in a day. You'll probably be surprised. Put water in a pitcher to keep track of drinking water and cooking water. Find out how much water you flush when you flush your toilet each time and estimate how much water per minute your shower puts out (test it by collecting water from your shower in a measured container for one minute). If you wash clothes, pay attention to how many gallons it takes. If you wash your car, put the water in a bucket first to measure it out. Estimate how many gallons go on your lawn or garden per minute by measuring the same way you did

Additional Layer

The concept of sustainability has been broadened to include political and economic aims like equality, education, and eradication of poverty, as well as environmental aims. It's pretty much, "Let's make the world perfect." It's the most ambitious set of goals ever.

Look up the UN sustainability goals to see what we mean.

On the Web

Biodiversity means the number of species in an environment. Greater numbers is generally considered better.

Watch "Why is Biodiversity so Important?" from TED Ed with your younger kids: https://youtu.be/GK_vRtHJZu4

Watch "Biodiversity" from Bozeman Science with your high schoolers: https://youtu.be/0-PE-3ve3w2w

Additional Layer

The Arabian oryx was extinct in the wild by the 1970s. It was reintroduced from captive populations and 1,000 are now in the wild. The Phoenix Zoo was the first zoo to ever use a captive breeding program.

Additional Layer

People are designing homes and buildings that are easier on the environment. They include things like better insulation, materials sourced sustainably, less harsh chemicals, and passive solar heating.

In passive solar design, buildings are made to use the sun's heat to warm them in winter and then to fend off the hot sun in the summer, keeping the building cooler.

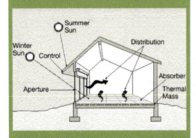

Learn more about passive solar design, zero net energy design, and other environmentally friendly building designs.

On the Web

What if you want to make conservation your career? Does that even exist? Yes, and it's a growing field.

Watch "Introduction to Conservation Science" where a conservation scientist talks about jobs: https://youtu.be/BO-HUX-DAdVE

for the shower. Keep a log all day long. At the end of the day, talk over what surprised you and what didn't. Discuss how you can be more careful of the water you use and use it more efficiently.

☺ ☺ EXPLORATION: Threatened Environments

Some environments are especially threatened because of human activity. Look up information on one of these places: Madagascar, Borneo, Micronesia, Madrean Sky Islands, or the Mediterranean Basin. Find out why these areas are important ecologically and why they are threatened.

Create a collage of images and words from the environment you researched. You could have pictures of animals and plants that are found in that place and words that tell what is threatening it.

☺ ☺ ☺ EXPERIMENT: Clean Air

The cleanliness of air is important to people as well as animals and plants. In this experiment you will see for yourself how clean the air is.

You need several microscope slides, petroleum jelly, and a microscope. Smear petroleum jelly on the surface of 5-8 microscope slides, completely covering one side of each slide. Place each slide in a different environment and let it sit there for 2-3 days. You might put one in your kitchen, one in your bedroom, one in your front yard, one in your back yard, one inside your car, and so on. Keep track of which slide is which and examine them under a microscope.

Write up your findings on an experiment sheet.

☺ ☺ ☺ EXPEDITION: Wildlife Rehabilitation Center

Wildlife rehabilitation centers provide care to wild animals that have been orphaned or injured so they can return to the wild. Wildlife rehabilitators have to have special licenses to operate. They also have to know first aid for animals and be educated about local species of wildlife.

There are wildlife rehabilitation centers all over the world in nearly every community. Find out if you can visit one near you for a field trip. Be prepared with a few good questions for the people at the center.

☺ ☺ EXPERIMENT: Clean Rivers and Streams

Water quality in streams, lakes, and rivers can be negatively impacted by things like sewage treatment plants, water runoff from roadways, agricultural runoff, and so on. You can test the cleanliness and health of water in a wild place near you. First, you need a test kit. You can get the "environmental testing lab kit" from Home Science Tools online (it also has materials for testing air quality). Or you can get a "pond test kit" from Amazon.com. A test kit should test for pH, nitrite, ammonia, and phosphate at the very least. Besides these things, test the stream temperature both on the surface and three feet down with a thermometer.

Run the test at several locations in your water system. Near my house I would test just below and above the local water treatment plant on our river, on a smaller tributary stream, near land by a farm, and in an area away from the town. Take pictures at your test locations.

Besides your tests, you might look up information online about any environmental concerns in the waterways you are testing.

Organize the data and information you found on a poster about the health of your local water.

☺ ☺ ☺ EXPERIMENT: Acid Rain and Plants

Acid rain is caused when sulfur dioxide and nitrogen oxide are released into the air by factories or automobiles. If the pH of rainwater drops below 5.7, it can have severe effects on plants and animals. Entire regions of forests and lakes can die. You can experiment with the effects of acid rain on plants.

You will need five identical plants, distilled water, pH test strips, and vinegar. You can get distilled water in the automotive section of stores. Science suppliers, pet stores, and Amazon all sell pH test strips.

1. Prepare five different solutions of water with different pH readings. Just add vinegar in varying amounts to distilled water. Note that normal rainwater can have pH readings down to 5.6. Use pH papers to test the pH of each water and vinegar solution. Mark the solutions with their pH.
2. Label each plant with its assigned pH and measure the height and width of each plant at the beginning of the experiment. Take a photo of each plant.
3. Water the plants with the same amount of water each day for three weeks, each with its assigned pH of water. Measure and photograph your plants each week.

Write up your findings about acid rain effects and use your photos and data in your report. Discuss the larger effects that acid rain would have on entire ecosystems over large swaths of land.

Fabulous Fact

Though conservation is a modern movement, people throughout history have been interested in wildlife and the health of nature.

Read up on St. Cuthbert and the Farne Islands to learn about the first bird sanctuary in the world.

Memorization Station

Look up and learn the definitions of these terms:

- Conservation
- Biodiversity
- Non-point source pollution
- Point source pollution
- Endangered species
- Extinction
- Endemic
- Sustainability

Additional Layer

Many people are very worried about climate change. If the earth's climate does change, either cooling or warming, this could have a dramatic effect on ecosystems.

Read about the problem here: http://science.howstuffworks.com/environmental/green-science/global-warming.htm

Then do more research and develop an opinion.

THE ARTS: CREATIVE KIDS

Famous Folks

Do some research and learn more about one of these highly creative people:

Albert Einstein

Thomas Edison

Nikola Tesla

Marie Curie

Vincent Van Gogh

Leonardo da Vinci

Alexander Graham Bell

Benjamin Franklin

Berthe Morisot

Richard Feynman

On The Web

You can design your own shirts online and then actually buy the shirt you designed. Just search for "t-shirt creators" or "design custom t-shirts" to find some sites that will make your designs reality.

Teaching Tip

You can use another set of favorite toys in place of Legos to create a stop motion. A train set, toy dinosaurs, cowboys and Indians, or your stuffed animals can all star in your stop motion film.

Each year of the Layers of Learning program includes one Creative Kids art unit. There are several components to a good art education. We focus a lot on art history, and that's the first component. The second is practical art skills - drawing, painting, sculpting, and more. We give you a start on that and hope that art-inclined kids will also be able to pursue lessons and private art instruction. The last component is creativity. Creative kids tend to be more curious, flexible, independent, and adventurous. They persist at tasks when others give up, because they are certain they will eventually discover a path to success. Creativity can be encouraged by allowing for freedom of expression. Don't give specific instructions. Tell your kids that there isn't always one right way to do things. Their ideas are valid. They can try things out for themselves to see if they succeed. Let them choose their own exploration to pursue from this unit, and if they have another creative idea, let them pursue that instead. The focus should be on independence and pursuit of inventive, artistic, creative ideas.

☺ ☺ ☺ EXPLORATION: Create a T-Shirt

There are lots of fun things you can use to decorate your own t-shirt. Begin with a plain t-shirt as your canvas. You could tie dye it, silkscreen it, do a bleach pen design, use fabric markers, design and apply t-shirt vinyl, or use permanent markers. This design was done using permanent markers and rubbing alcohol. The alcohol partially dissolves the ink, allowing it to run. Before you wash it, run over the t-shirt with an iron to set your design.

☺ ☺ ☺ EXPLORATION: Lego Stop Motion

Write, direct, photograph, and produce your own Lego stop motion production. Build a Lego scene and set your character(s) in it. Take a photograph. Then slightly adjust the character's position over and over, photographing each time. Have your character "act out" a whole scene or storyline, with you photographing his or her every move. Once you're finished, put the photographs in order in a simple slide show that plays quickly. You'll be able to watch the scene unfold.

☺ ☻ EXPLORATION: Make a Garden or Fairy Garden

Make your own children's garden or fairy garden. This can be as small and simple as a flowerpot garden or big and sprawling if you've got the land and space to do it in.

Rather than just buying components, gather and make some items for your garden. You can make small houses out of decorated 2

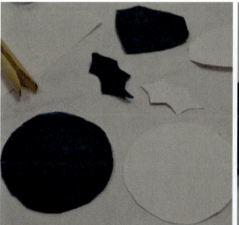
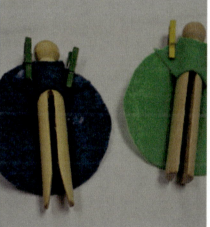

Additional Layer

If you're looking for a creative project that continues on, you might consider starting Project 365. It can take many forms, but essentially, you will document each day of your life for one year, or 365 days. This could mean taking a photo of something you do each day to put in a photo album and journal about, or it might just be writing something that happened to you on an index card and filing it in a card file. Usually it includes some form of scrapbooking or doodling to showcase your personality as well. At the end, you have a portrait of your year.

Additional Layer

Make a Superbowl commercial. Choose any product you want to advertise and come up with a great idea for an entertaining commercial that the fans will get behind. Companies try to play their best commercials during the Superbowl because they know there are so many people watching. The advertising fees are high during the big game, so make sure your commercial is the best it can be. Film it and show it to an audience.

Teaching Tip

If you have more than one team for a treasure hunt, it is best if they start out in different places so they aren't following each other through the whole hunt. You can use all the same clues, but have them progress in a different order so the two teams will be independently solving them. Color code the clues and tell the team they are to collect only the clues that match their team's color.

Additional Layer

Rather than a kite, younger kids might enjoy crafting a simple windsock. Don't be limited by the traditional windsock shape. Just cut out two identical shapes. Attach them with an empty toilet paper tube in between. Staple all around the edges. Then lace a ribbon through it and tie it off at the top, leaving the ribbons tailing out the bottom for extra decoration. Add a staple on the ribbon and windsock at the bottom to secure it.

liter bottles or milk cartons. Incorporate natural items like rocks and sticks. Craft your own fairies using wooden clothespins.

☺ ☺ ☺ EXPLORATION: Treasure or Scavenger Hunt

Design, create, and host your own treasure or scavenger hunt. Invite friends or family to play your game with you when you are done. This would make a really fun family night too.

For a treasure hunt you'll need to write clues, one that leads to the next, and hide them ahead of time. Make sure to hide a treasure at the end. You can make your clues extra clever by making them rhyme or incorporating little puzzles, riddles, or math problems that must be solved in order to decipher the clues.

For a scavenger hunt, you'll create a list of items each team must find. They can either be required to gather the items, or just take pictures of them. You can have really specific items (a pair of shoes, a red flower, a boat) or more vague options (something that has been lost, a yellow item in the park, something sticky). The game is a race to see who can gather or photograph all of their items the fastest and then return for the prize.

☺ ☺ EXPLORATION: Fly A Kite

Design and build your own kite. Use tissue paper or plastic garbage bags, wooden dowels, and kite string or embroidery floss. You may want to add a tail or other components as well. It may take you several tries to get a design that actually flies. We used a combination of hot glue, wood glue, and super glue on our kites, along with wooden dowels and plastic garbage sacks.

☺ ☻ ☺ **EXPLORATION: Plan A Dream Vacation**

As you're planning your dream vacation, remember that even the sky is not the limit! It could be a terrestrial trip, but you could also be going to the moon or even Saturn! You might stay at a hotel at the bottom of the ocean or go parasailing in the highest lake in the world, Lake Titicaca. You can make this as imaginative and creative as you would like. Create an itinerary, complete with pictures, of your dream vacation.

☺ ☻ ☺ **EXPLORATION: Animal Creator**

Make a list of a few of your favorite animals. Combine the animals in interesting ways in pictures you draw. You might have a kangaroo with a lion's mane and an elephant's trunk. Or you could have a sheep with an giraffe's long neck and a dog's tail. Create your own cool animal combinations.

☺ ☻ ☺ **EXPLORATION: Egg Drop Challenge**

Engineer a container for an egg so that when you drop it, the egg won't break. Limit yourself to things you have found, not that you have to purchase. Use your imagination and your science know-how to think of the perfect way to protect your egg. Craft the container and put your egg inside. Go to a place that has a second story that you can safely drop it from. Drop your container and see if your egg survived the fall without cracking.

☺ ☻ ☺ **EXPLORATION: Sun Catchers**

You can design your own sun catchers using pony beads. Begin with a glass baking dish. Preheat your oven to 400 degrees. Set the pony beads on your glass baking dish in any design you like. You can either freehand a design or use a cookie cutter as an outline and fill it up. Silicone molds work well as an outline too, and are easy for little fingers to fill with pony beads. Make your creation just one bead deep, but fill that layer completely. Put the baking dish in the preheated oven and bake it for 30 minutes. The pony beads

Additional Layer

Arranging flowers is kind of like the Animal Creator Exploration. Florists take many kinds of flowers and combine them in interesting ways into one bouquet. Try making your own flower arrangement. If possible, arrange with a local florist to take a lesson first, and then start making a bouquet you like.

Additional Layer

Make your own cookie recipe. Read five to ten cookie recipes, trying to spot the basics of what they have in common. Then write your own cookie recipe with flavor combinations you think you would like. Mix up a batch of your cookies, bake them, and try them out. Did they turn out the way you had hoped?

Recipe developers often make many versions before they get it just right. You might have to tweak yours and try it more than once!

will melt together into one mass. Remove from the oven and let them cool. Once they are cool you can apply just a bit of pressure and they will pop right off of the glass baking dish. Hot glue a small fishing line loop on to the top so you can hang your sun catchers in the window.

😊 😊 😊 EXPLORATION: Huge Chalk Art Mural

Go outside and make a huge chalk art mural. You'll need lots of colorful chalks, a water bottle, and blending rags. It can also be helpful to bring coloring books or printed simple outline drawings to look at as you create your chalk sketches.

Writer's Workshop

Computer programming and robotics are creative fields. Programmers and engineers are constantly trying to push technology further and invent the next big thing. Make a list of some cool things you wish your cell phone, computer, or smartwatch could do. Do you think those things will one day be possible?

EXPLANATION: The Opposite of Creativity

In order to understand creativity better, we can look at what some opposites of creativity and the creative process are.

- The opposite of a creator is a destroyer. Someone who is destructive is tearing down while someone who is creative is building up.
- Another opposite process is automation. Someone who is doing something automatically, without thinking, is being the opposite of creative. Creativity involves differing from the norm.
- Mindlessness is another opposite of creativity. When we are going about life mindlessly, we are not creating. Creating must include engaged thinking and problem solving.
- Anxiety can keep us from being creative. Anxiousness and pessimism do not lead to creation, but rather, put our mind in a stall. Creative people tend to be optimistic problem solvers.

Keeping those ideas in mind, how can we encourage creativity? We can help kids become more creative by presenting authentic problems to solve, but not feeding them the answers. This could be applied to making a t-shirt or a new recipe as readily as coming up with a new invention or a STEM challenge. In each case, we are presenting a task and the tools necessary to complete it, but not providing step by step instructions. Kids must be allowed to think on their own, develop their own plan, and come to their own conclusions.

Throughout the problem solving time, we can scaffold them by staying positive, expressing our confidence in them, and pointing out the strengths they have that will lead them to creative answers. If we stop them in the middle and tell them why their ideas won't work or how we think they could improve on them, this immediately stops their creative process. In the long run, it causes them to revert to relying on others mindlessly and becoming anxious about being wrong. On the other hand, if they come to those conclusions on their own and apply what they've learned, they can continue to create, even if it takes them longer and involves many failures along the way.

☺ ☺ ☺ EXPLORATION: Tall Tower Challenge

Set out dry spaghetti noodles and marshmallows in a variety of sizes and challenge your kids to create the tallest tower they can in 20 minutes. Begin by giving them 5 minutes of practice and planning time before the official 20 minutes begins. They can experiment with the structure and how to best get the marshmallows and noodles to stay together. Then begin the timer with 20 minutes. At the end of the 20 minutes, compare all of the towers

Fabulous Fact

My son recently attended an electronics convention with an inventor who was describing his creative process. Someone asked, "How did you learn to think outside the box?" He replied, "When I was five years old I took my box out to the back yard and burned it."

Fabulous Fact

Most creative people spend time doing these four things every single day:

1. Reading
2. Meditating
3. Writing
4. Talking with people

Writer's Workshop

One of the keys to success in creative endeavors is not being afraid to fail. Some of the greatest minds in history failed over and over again before accomplishing great things.

Write about something you hope to accomplish and whether or not you are afraid to fail. How will you pursue your goals regardless of failures?

On The Web

STEM challenges are terrific creative endeavors. Like the egg drop challenge and the Tall Tower Challenge, kids are presented with a task in the realm of science, technology, engineering, or mathematics. They are provided with supplies, but need to figure out how to accomplish the task creatively.

The Layers of Learning STEM Pinterest Board has lots of additional ideas for STEM challenges for kids.

https://www.pinterest.com/layerslearning/stem/

Writer's Workshop

Bedtime notebooks are a great way for creative people to keep track of things. Keep a notebook by your bed and write or draw in it before bedtime. Record your ideas and the problems you are working on solving. Your brain will work on them while you sleep. Wake up and write your new ideas.

and name the winner based on the tallest part of the tower they have standing. If a tower falls down, even if it was taller than another, it doesn't count. It must be standing when the time elapses. Have a prize prepared for the winner.

☺ ☺ ☺ EXPLORATION: Theme Dinner

Plan a theme dinner. The theme can be anything. Plan and create fitting decorations, make a menu, and cook food that goes along with your theme. Set up the dinner table, prepare the food, and serve your guests.

Here are some ideas for themes you might like to try:
• Wild West Round-up

- Under the Sea
- Colonial Dinner
- Sports (or another activity of interest)
- Science
- Holiday of your choice
- Country Spotlight (Choose a country to base your meal around)
- Storybook Dinner (based on a book you've read)
- Fairy Tale Dinner
- Favorite Movie Feast
- Medieval Feast
- Jungle Dinner
- Tropical Island Paradise/Luau
- Ancient Times Dinner

Remember to be creative. Think of your own ideas and create your own vision for your theme dinner.

☺ ☺ ☺ EXPLORATION: Art Potluck

Set a variety of materials out on a table, anything from clean, used food containers, shoe boxes, and plastic cups to pipe cleaners, wiggly eyes, and pony beads. Have each kid make their own art piece using every single "ingredient" on the table. Make sure to have some basic art tools available too - scissors, glue, and other basic supplies that can be used, but don't have to be incorporated into the art project.

Additional Layer

Every day for a week, find something old in your house and give it a makeover to make it better or reuse it in some way.

Teaching Tip

Sometimes the seed of creativity is having a goal or dream. Have your kids brainstorm some things they dream of doing in whatever field they are interested in. It's far better to have too many dreams than not enough. Have your kids write down their dreams. Whether or not they accomplish them all, they will appreciate the list later. And if they lack a dream, sometimes in the absence of a dream or passion, curiosity will be enough. Encourage your kids to be curious and then creatively pursue their curiosity.

Coming up next:

My ideas for this unit:

Title: _____ **Topic:** _____

_____

_____

_____

_____

_____

_____

_____

_____

_____

Title: _____ **Topic:** _____

_____

_____

_____

_____

_____

_____

_____

_____

_____

Title: _____ **Topic:** _____

_____

_____

_____

_____

_____

_____

_____

_____

_____

Title: _____   **Topic:** _____

_____

_____

_____

_____

_____

_____

_____

_____

_____

_____

Title: _____   **Topic:** _____

_____

_____

_____

_____

_____

_____

_____

_____

_____

_____

Title: _____   **Topic:** _____

_____

_____

_____

_____

_____

_____

_____

_____

_____

_____

Terrorism Memorial

This is a sculpture that is on the campus at the University of Dhaka in Bangladesh. It was built in 1995 to remember Moin Hossain Raju, a student at the university who was killed by terrorists because he was protesting terror. It shows how the students came together both before and after the attack to stand against the methods of hatred and fear.

Terrorism Timeline

May 1970
Avivim school bus RPG attack in Israel, killing and maiming 31 children and adults.

Sept. 5, 1972
Nine Israeli athletes are taken hostage and killed by the Black September Arab terrorist group at the Munich Olympics.

August 1978
A fire set in the Cinema Rex, Abadan, Iran kills 470 people.

Nov. 4, 1979
The American embassy in Tehran, Iran was attacked, 66 Americans are taken hostage and held for 444 days.

June 1985
Air India flight 182 downed in first airplane bombing, 329 people killed by Babbar Khalsa.

1985
11 Americans kidnapped off the streets of Beirut by the newly founded Hezbolla; Terry Anderson, the longest held, wasn't released until 1991

Dec. 21, 1988
Pan Am flight 103 explodes over Lockerbie, Scotland; 259 passengers and 11 people on the ground are killed. The Libyan government is responsible.

March 1993
A series of 12 bombings in Mumbai, India by D-Company kill 257 and injure 717.

September 1999
A series of four terrorist attacks by Caucasus Islamic Institute on Russian apartment buildings killed 293 and injured more than 1000.

Sept. 11, 2001
The World Trade center in New York and the Pentagon in Washington DC are attacked by terrorists with planes; 3000 dead

Oct. 2001
The U.S. retaliates for 9-11 by bombing Taliban and al-Qaeda in Afghanistan thus launching the "War on Terror"

Sept. 2004
Chechen terrorists attacked a school in Beslan, Russia. More than 300 people died in the three day siege, most of them children.

August 2007
Four coordinated suicide bombs killed 500 and injured 1500 in Yazidi communities in Iraq.

April 2014
276 girls from a school in Chibok, Nigeria kidnapped by Boko Haram.

May 2014
Towns of Gamboru and Ngala, Nigeria attacked by Boko Haram. 336 people killed.

July 2016
341 killed, more injured in the neighborhood of Karrada, Baghdad by Islamic State.

Photos shared under CC license on Wikimedia.

Worldwide Terror

Countries with the most frequent terrorist attacks in the early 21st century

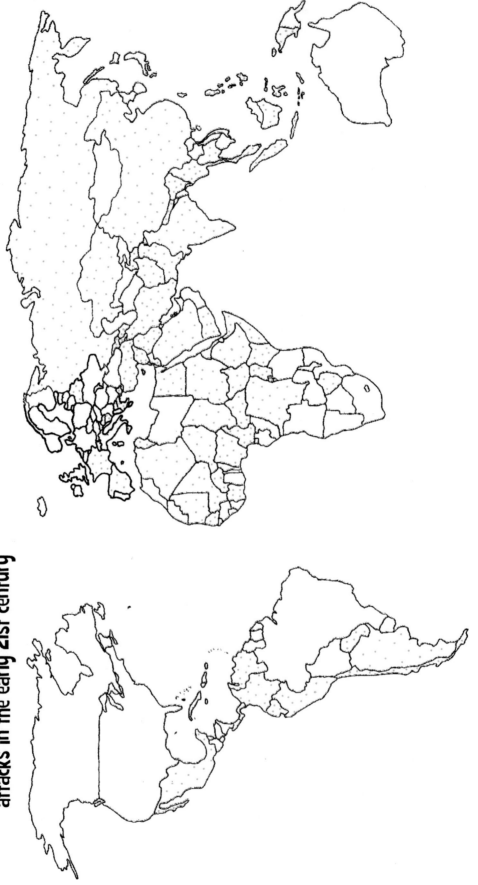

This Is Terrorism

17 July 2009
Jakarta

13 Nov. 2015
Paris

15 Sept. 2008
Morelia

14-17 Dec. 2009
Makombo

30 July 1990
East Sussex

16 Feb. 2017
Sehwan

A Guide To Airport Safety

1. Have several forms of ID and make sure they match your ticket

2. Remove your shoes at checkpoints

3. All baggage and people must be screened

4. No liquids over 3.4 oz.

5. Toiletries must be removed from bags and checked at checkpoints

6. Remove outerwear at checkpoints

7. You may be taken out of line randomly for a search

8. Only ticketed travelers may go past security checkpoints

9. Cockpit doors stay locked during flights

Does airport security keep us safe?

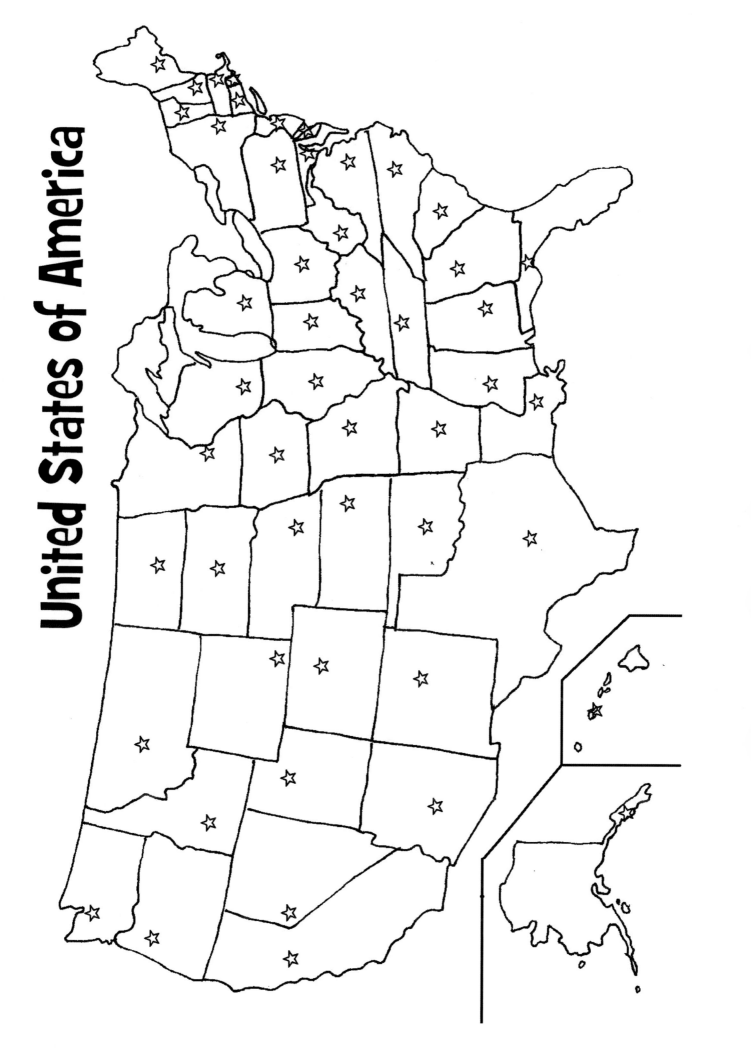

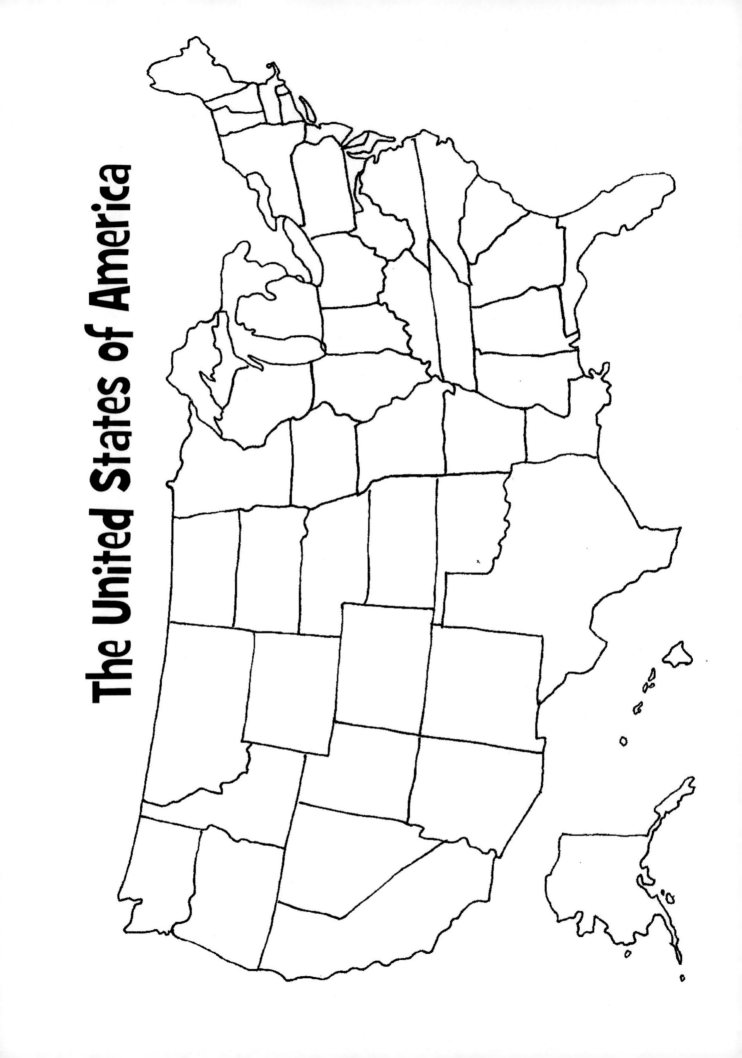

The United States of America

U.S.A.

Fill in this map with as many details as you can remember about the landscape. Put Washington D.C. in the right spot.

Statue of Liberty

Angel Falls

Gateway Arch

Golden Gate Bridge

Grand Canyon

Liberty Bell

Old Faithful

Shanghai Tower

Mount Rushmore

Niagara Falls

St. Peter's Basilica

White House

Sunday	Monday	Tuesday	Wednesday	Thursday	Friday	Saturday

Who Belongs on the Dollar Bill?

What important American has made a big difference to this country who has earned their spot on the dollar bill? Choose a modern or historical American who has never been on real U.S. currency to draw into the dollar bill below. Then write about the accomplishments that made him or her worthy of this honor.

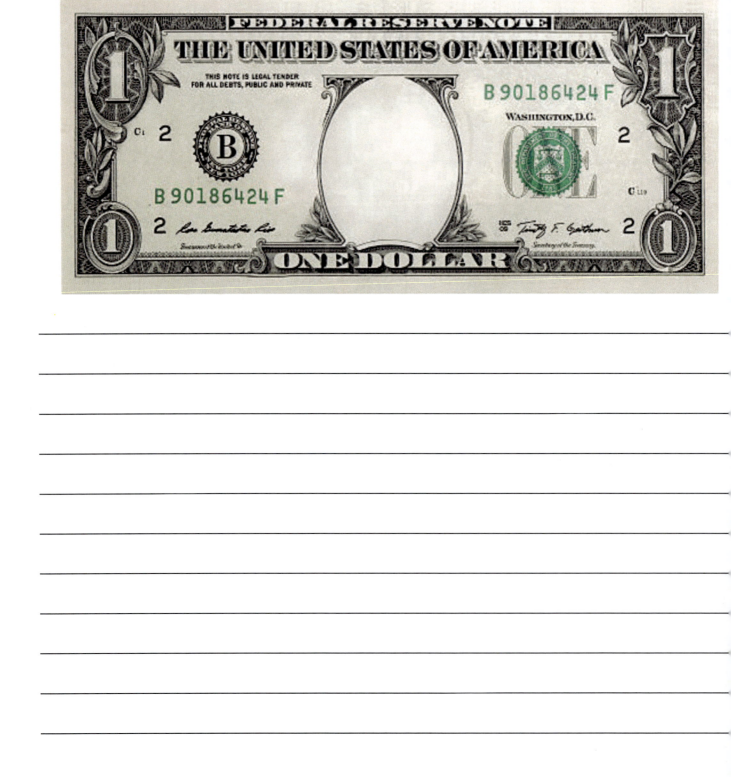

_____

_____

_____

_____

_____

_____

_____

_____

_____

About the Authors

Karen & Michelle . . .
Mothers, sisters, teachers, women who are passionate
about educating kids.
We are dedicated to lifelong learning.

Karen, a mother of four, who has homeschooled her kids for more than eight years with her husband, Bob, has a bachelor's degree in child development with an emphasis in education. She lives in Idaho, gardens, teaches piano, and plays an excruciating number of board games with her kids. Karen is our resident arts expert and English guru {most necessary as Michelle regularly and carelessly mangles the English language and occasionally steps over the bounds of polite society}.

Michelle and her husband, Cameron, have homeschooled their six boys for more than a decade. Michelle earned a bachelors in biology, making her the resident science expert, though she is mocked by her friends for being the Botanist with the Black Thumb of Death. She also is the go-to for history and government. She believes in staying up late, hot chocolate, and a no whining policy. We both pitch in on geography, in case you were wondering.

Visit our constantly updated blog for tons of free ideas,
free printables, and more cool stuff for sale:
www.Layers-of-Learning.com

Made in the USA
Middletown, DE
04 April 2025

73769578R00031